NORTH AMERICAN WILDLIFE

AMERICAN BEAVERS

by Jenny Mason

Kaleidoscope
Minneapolis, MN

The Quest for Discovery Never Ends

This edition first published in 2024 by Kaleidoscope Publishing, Inc.

For information regarding permission, write to
Kaleidoscope Publishing, Inc.
6012 Blue Circle Drive
Minnetonka, MN 55343

Library of Congress Control Number
2023936905

ISBN
978-1-64519-721-8 (library bound)
978-1-64519-769-0 (ebook)

Printed in the United States of America.

Bigfoot lurks within one of the images in this book. It's up to you to find him!

TABLE OF CONTENTS

Chapter 1

BUILDING A LIFE

Dusk is peaceful in the forest. Crickets chirp. Frogs in a pond croak. *Snap!* A tree trunk breaks like a bone. *Whoosh! Wham!* It falls to the ground. Startled birds fly away. Wood chips ring the tree stump. A beaver waddles through them to the tree it cut down. No time to rest. She has much to build. Beavers do not just live in a **habitat**. They design and build their spaces. Humans also do this. Both beaver and human projects are visible from outer space. No other animals change the world so much.

Space satellites found the world's largest beaver dam. It spans 2,800 feet (850 m). That is twice the length of the Hoover Dam in Nevada.

The beaver drags the tree using her teeth. She lugs it to a watery ditch, or canal. Beavers build canals, dams, and lodges. Canals act as roads. Beavers swim through them to quickly get food or supplies. The beaver floats the tree down the canal. She takes it to the pond she created. To make ponds, beavers dam streams. They jam cut logs into the mud. The logs point upstream. They pin the logs with heavy rocks. Then, they pack in branches, grass, and mud. People need work crews and machines to build dams. Beavers work alone or in pairs.

The largest tree chopped down by a beaver was about 150 feet (45 m) tall. That is about as tall as the Arc de Triomphe in Paris.

Dusk darkens into night. The beaver repairs the dam with the new tree. Next, she must work on the lodge. Beavers live in lodges. Some are built on the bank of the pond. Others form an island in the water. Lodges look like a heap of sticks. Actually, the sticks and mud are woven together like an upside-down nest. Lodges are strong. Not even bears can bust them open. Beavers build a cozy apartment inside. It sits above the water. Shredded wood forms the floor. The door is a watery tunnel. It is like an indoor swimming pool!

CHAIN SAWS THAT CHEW

Beavers are like chewing chain saws. Their four front teeth are called incisors. They are very sharp. Beavers stab their top teeth into the tree. Next, they pull their bottom teeth up. Their jaws are powerful. The bottom teeth carve out wood chunks. A beaver can chop a six-inch (15-cm) tree trunk in 20 minutes.

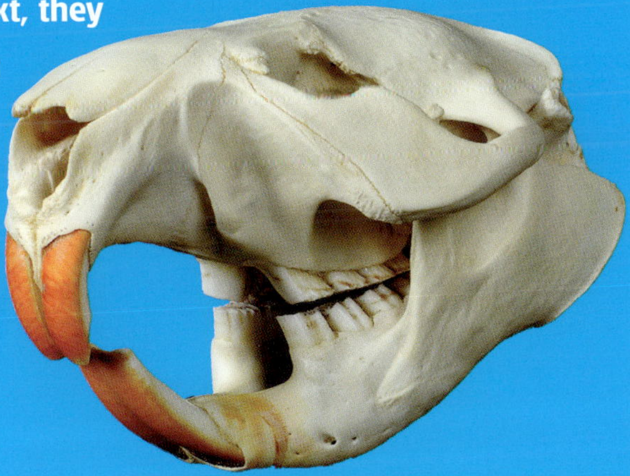

Chapter 2

BORN TO SWIM

Light is hazy underwater. Sounds are muffled. The water is cold. Ponds are murky worlds. A beaver glides through this world. He is a born swimmer. All beavers are semi-aquatic. That means they live mostly in water. Ponds hide them from **predators**. Their back paws are webbed like duck feet. But beavers are not birds. They are **rodents**, like squirrels, mice, woodchucks, and porcupines. Beavers are North America's largest rodent. They are the second largest rodent in the world. Capybaras are bigger. Beavers range across Alaska and Canada. They live in forests across the United States.

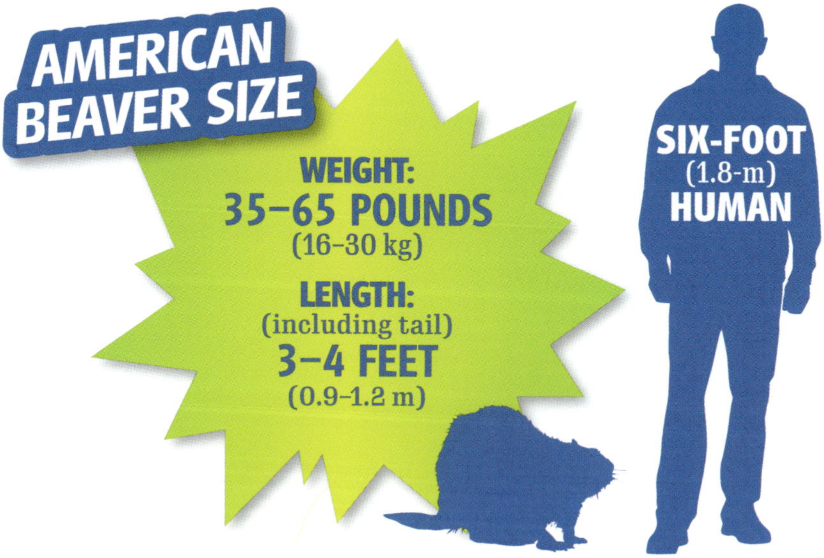

Where Do AMERICAN BEAVERS Live?

The beaver rises to the surface. His nose, ears, and eyes barely poke out of the water. He watches some hikers. They have stopped at his pond to relax. They cannot see him. Beavers are sneaky. He dives underwater. He can hold his breath for three to five minutes. He can stretch it to 15 minutes. Beaver lungs are large. They have built-in swim goggles, too. A thin, clear **tissue** covers their eyes as they swim. Beaver fur is the perfect swimsuit. Fuzzy fur near the skin traps air. This air pocket keeps the beaver warm. Longer hairs shield the fuzz from water.

FURRY RAINCOAT

A beaver's fur is like a raincoat. It is waterproof. Beavers produce a special oil. They rub this oil over their long outer coat. Oil drives away water. Beavers have a trick to dry off fast. The hind paws have a split claw. They use it like a comb. It scrapes water off the fur.

The hikers are gone. The beaver waddles out of the pond. It chops down a sapling. It nibbles on the soft bark. The beaver's teeth do not help it swim. But they do help it survive. The incisors never stop growing. Constant use wears them down. Enamel covers the front of the teeth. It is a rock-hard substance. This enamel has iron mixed in. It adds strength. It also turns the teeth bright orange.

Stomachs are not great at digesting wood. Beavers have a special gut, or caecum, to help. Beavers leave two kinds of **scat**. Green mush comes from the caecum. Beavers eat this mush. The other scat is like sawdust marbles.

FUN FACT

Ancient people used beaver teeth or bones for tools. The incisors make excellent chisels.

Chapter 3

BUSY AS BEAVERS

Dawn glows pink over the pond. A beaver family is already at work. They tend to leaks in the dam. They patch up the lodge. Beavers are active in the morning and evening.

A bear stalks the pond. Maybe it can sneak up on the beavers. *Ker-splash!* The sudden noise scares the bear. It runs away. Beavers slap their tails on water when they see predators. The splash is a warning to hide. Wolves, coyotes, bobcats, and eagles are some common beaver predators. Successful beavers live 8 to 10 years. Beaver couples **mate** for life.

Beaver tails are made of keratin. In humans, keratin makes hair and nails.

Beavers are busy all spring and summer. In April, babies, or kits, are born in **litters**. A typical litter has two to four kits. Within a few days, kits can swim. Their older siblings help babysit.

Yearlings leave the family at age two. They must find a mate. The whole family helps with building projects. Mother beavers and their young feast. Willow, rowan, and aspen trees are favorites. So are water lilies. Male beavers patrol their **territory**. They build mud mounds. They squirt castoreum on the mounds. This yellow-gray liquid smells like vanilla.

FUN FACT

People once used castoreum in perfumes, foods, and makeup. The liquid is mostly beaver urine.

In autumn, something strange happens. Floating tree branches dive into the pond. Hidden underwater, beavers tug the branches. They ram them into mud near the lodge. This will be their food for winter. Think of it as a beaver refrigerator. Beavers can gather one ton (907 kg) or more of food. These animals are busy all winter. They do not **hibernate**. They are very warm in the lodge. If the pond does not freeze, they will gather twigs to eat.

SPEAK BEAVER

Beavers communicate using sounds. Kits whine for food. They whine if a sibling will not play. Adults hiss to scare away other beavers. They also chatter their teeth. Other animals hear this sound as a warning. Growls send a clear message: a beaver is about to attack.

Chapter 4

LEAVE IT TO BEAVERS

A plane roars over the state of Idaho. Boxes trickle out of its cargo hold. Parachutes open. The boxes clunk to the ground. When they open, dazed beavers crawl out. In the 1940s, these beaver bombs relocated beavers far away from towns. Beaver habitats ruin roads. They flood farms. They damage homes. People struggle to see how beavers are a benefit.

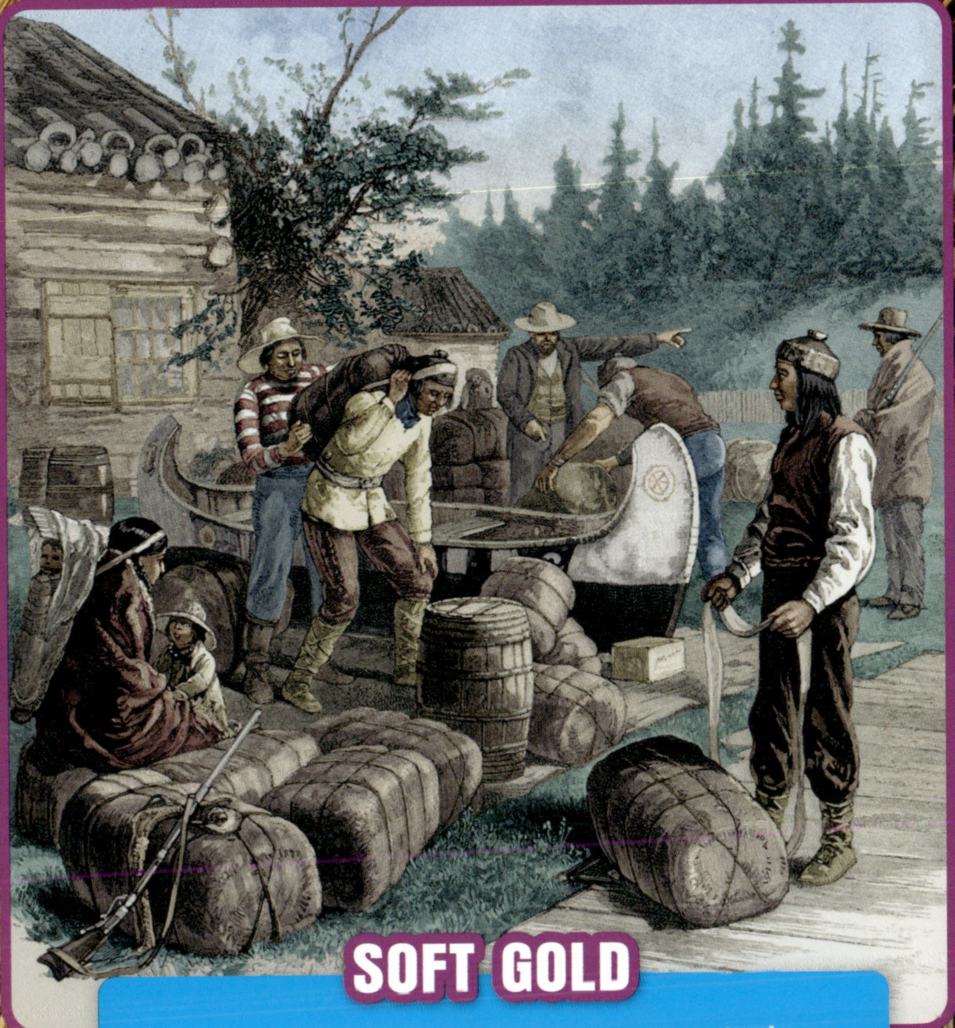

SOFT GOLD

Some people consider beavers to be pests. In the past, they were a rich prize. Beaver fur made the best hats. Countries fought wars for the fur. In 1871, the Hudson's Bay Company sold more than 174,000 fur pelts. North America's beaver population crashed. Sixty to 400 million beavers shrank to 100,000. Today, there are about 15 million.

Sunlight sparkles on the beaver pond. The beavers nap inside the lodge. Around them, pond life buzzes. Floating geese honk. Ducks quack. Fish jump from the water to catch flies. Turtles sunbathe on the dam. Beaver ponds support other animals. Half of North America's **endangered** species cannot survive without beavers. Ponds and canals create wetlands. These areas are rich with food sources. Healthy soils build up. Plants and trees grow stronger.

Duck populations are 75 percent larger in areas where beavers live.

Recent studies show that beavers benefit people too. In 2018, a wildfire swept across Idaho. It burned 65,000 acres (26,000 ha). Beaver wetlands survived the fire. They were lush and green. They protected other animals from the flames. Thank goodness for those “beaver bombs.”

Beaver wetlands fight climate change. They act as air conditioners on hot days. Wetlands are also a water source during a **drought**. Beavers reshape landscapes. When an old dam breaks, the pond becomes a swamp. The swamp dries into a meadow. The meadow sprouts a forest with streams to dam. No wonder beavers are busy. They are part of a mighty cycle.

BEYOND THE BOOK

After reading the book, it's time to think about what you learned. Try the following exercises to jump-start your ideas.

THINK

FIND OUT MORE. Get busy learning about beavers. There is so much more to discover about them. What else do you want to know? Look them up on the web, or check out a book from the library. Visit a national park or wildlife ranger station in areas where beavers live to learn more.

CREATE

ART TIME. Can you draw a beaver? Look up a picture and grab some markers and paper. Which beaver structure will you draw? What is your beaver busy doing? Maybe it is chopping a tree or swimming. The sky is the limit!

SHARE

THE MORE YOU KNOW. Share what you learned about the North American beaver. Use your own words to write a paragraph. What are the main ideas of this book? What facts from the book can you use to support those ideas? Share your paragraph with a classmate. Do they have any comments or questions?

GROW

HELP OUT! Many animals around the world are struggling to survive. Find an organization that is trying to save your favorite animal. Can you volunteer? Can your family donate to the organization's mission? You can also help by telling people about the animal. The more people who help, the more the animal can be protected.

RESEARCH NINJA

Visit www.ninjaresearcher.com/7218 to learn how to take your research skills and book report writing to the next level!

DIGITAL LITERACY TOOLS

Research

SEARCH LIKE A PRO
Learn how to use search engines to find useful websites.

FACT OR FAKE
Discover how you can tell a trusted website from an untrustworthy resource.

TEXT DETECTIVE
Explore how to zero in on the information you need most.

SHOW YOUR WORK
Research responsibly—learn how to cite sources.

DOWNLOADABLE BOOK REPORT FORMS

Write

GET TO THE POINT
Learn how to express your main ideas.

PLAN OF ATTACK
Learn prewriting exercises and create an outline.

Further Resources

BOOKS

Holland, Mary. *The Beavers' Busy Year*. Mount Pleasant, SC: Arbordale, 2014.

Riggs, Kate. *Beavers*. Mankato, MN: The Creative Company, 2023.

Silverman, Buffy. *Wetlands*. Chicago, IL: Raintree, 2013.

WEBSITES

FACTSURFER

Factsurfer.com gives you a safe, fun way to find more information.

1. Go to www.factsurfer.com.
2. Enter "American Beavers" into the search box and click
3. Select your book cover to see a list of related websites.

Glossary

drought: A long period without rain

endangered: In danger of becoming extinct

habitat: The place where an animal or plant is usually found

hibernate: To sleep for the winter to survive cold temperatures and limited food supplies

litters: The groups of baby animals that are born at the same time to the same mother

mate: To join together to produce babies

predators: Animals that hunt and eat other animals

rodents: Mammals with large, sharp front teeth that constantly grow

scat: Wild animal poop

territory: The area an animal lives in and protects

tissue: A mass of similar cells that form a particular part or organ of an animal or plant

About the Author

Jenny Mason is a story-hunter. She explores foreign countries, canyon mazes, and burial crypts to gather the facts that make the best true tales. She received an MFA in Writing for Children and Young Adults from the Vermont College of Fine Arts. She also holds an MPhil from Trinity College Dublin. You will often find her hiking in the Colorado woods where beavers build worlds.

Index

PHOTO CREDITS

The images in this book are reproduced through the courtesy of: Jody Ann/Shutterstock Images, cover; Christian Musat/Shutterstock Images, p. 3; Sketchart/Shutterstock Images, p. 4 (circle); GatisVil/Shutterstock Images, p. 4–5; Gail Johnson/Shutterstock Images, p. 6; D. Gordon E. Robertson/Wikimedia Commons, p. 7 (top); Viereck/Shutterstock Images, p. 7 (bottom); Viktor Hejna/Shutterstock Images, p. 8 (top); Astrid Gast/Shutterstock Images, p. 8 (circle); Butler Stock Photography/Shutterstock Images, p. 9 (top); Audrey Snider-Bell/Shutterstock Images, p. 9 (skull); Justin Russ/Shutterstock Images, p. 12; KamalaNPS/Shutterstock Images, p. 13; Annette Shaff/ Shutterstock Images, p. 14; U. Eisenlohr/Shutterstock Images, p. 15; Josh Bukoski 1/Shutterstock Images, p. 16; Zadiraka Evgenii/Shutterstock Images, p. 17 (bottom); P Harstela/Shutterstock Images, p. 17 (top); UbjsP/Shutterstock Images, p. 18; Rejean Aline Bedard/Shutterstock Images, p. 19 (bottom); Litvalifa/Shutterstock Images, p. 19 (top); Iussiya/Shutterstock Images, p. 20; Dan-Pepper/Shutterstock Images, p. 21; Jordan Feeg/Shutterstock Images, p. 22; nik93737/Shutterstock Images, p. 23 (background); Henry Alexander Ogden (Harry Ogden)/Wikimedia Commons, p. 23; Pazyuk/Shutterstock Images, p. 24; Photo Spirit/Shutterstock Images, p. 24–25; Charles Knowles/ Shutterstock Images, p. 26–27; Jody Ann/Shutterstock Images, p. 31.